Presented to

_____

from

_____

MW00679282

A cheerful heart inside will show
An outward beauty that's sure to glow.

I Celebrate You!

Illustrated by Joy Marie 🌸 Written by J. J. Mills

Published by J. Countryman
a division of Thomas Nelson, Inc., Nashville, Tennessee 37214

Project Editor – Terri Gibbs

Designed by Starletta Polster, Murfreesboro, Tennessee

ISBN: 0-8499-5692-7

www.jcountryman.com

Printed in China

Plant friendship,
harvest happiness!

Our friendship has given
My life a new view,
With the joy I see
I celebrate
You!

JMills

I celebrate YOU

One of the things I appreciate
most about you is

_____

_____

_____

_____

_____

Nonsense among friends makes perfect Sense

T.J.Mills

I celebrate your HUMOR

Friends fill the hours with

sunshine and flowers

I celebrate your **Faithfulness**

Close to my heart
you'll always be,
friends forever
you and me.

A Friend that's true
is a friend all through
T.J. Mills

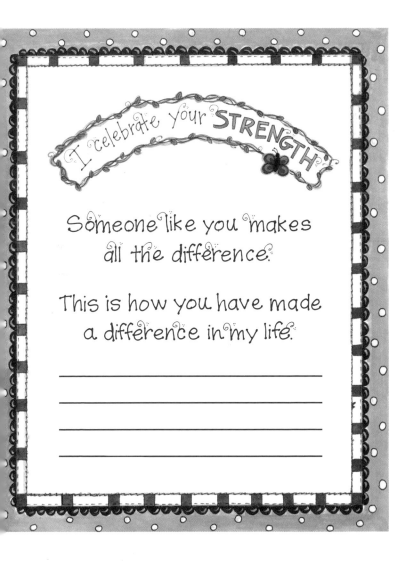

I celebrate your STRENGTH

Someone like you makes
all the difference.

This is how you have made
a difference in my life.

_____

_____

_____

_____

A true friend
will listen to what
no one else wants to hear

TJMills

JoyMarie ©

I celebrate your **KINDNESS**

Friendship fills an empty spot
you didn't know was there,
with dreams, hope, happiness,
and tender loving care.

The heart of Friendship

beats with acceptance

T.Mills

©JoyMarie

I celebrate your UNDERSTANDING

You make
my heart smile!

The arms of friendship hold a warm embrace

T.J. Mills

Joy Marie

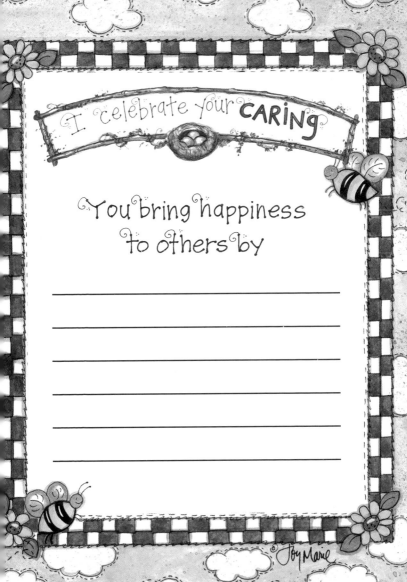

I celebrate your CARING

You bring happiness
to others by

_____

_____

_____

_____

_____

_____

JoyMarie

The seeds of great accomplishment are often nurtured through friendship

T. J. Mills

Sunflower

Wildflower Seeds

© Joy Marie

I celebrate your Encouragement

Take hold of each minute
put your whole soul in it and
breath deeply of life's bouquet.

With love,
all things grow;
with dreams,
all things are
possible.

May all your dreams
have their day.

I celebrate your **Companionship**

I'd like to give you a standing ovation for

_____

_____

_____

_____

_____

_____

Be yourself—it's someone
no one else can be,

do the best that you can do...
God will give you strength
and will bless you, too.

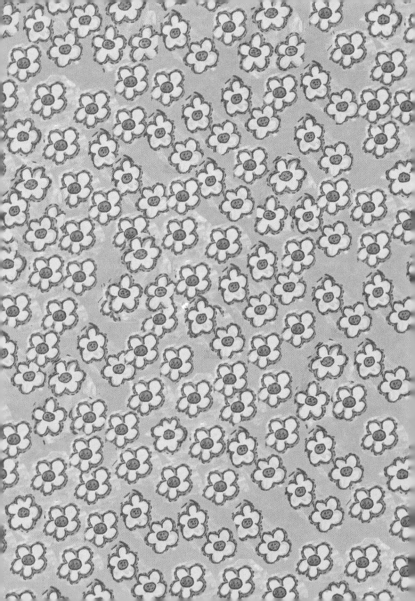